Report to the Department of the Interior

MARY BURRITT CHRISTIANSEN POETRY SERIES
Hilda Raz, Series Editor

The Mary Burritt Christiansen Poetry Series publishes two
to four books a year that engage and give voice to the
realities of living, working, and experiencing the West and
the Border as places and as metaphors. The purpose of the
series is to expand access to, and the audience for, quality
poetry, both single volumes and anthologies, that can be
used for general reading as well as in classrooms.

Mary Burritt
Christiansen
Poetry Series

Also available in the Mary Burritt Christiansen Poetry
Series:

The Arranged Marriage: Poems by Jehanne Dubrow
The Sky Is Shooting Blue Arrows: Poems by Glenna Luschei
A Selected History of Her Heart: Poems by Carole Simmons Oles
The Goldilocks Zone by Kate Gale
Flirt by Noah Blaustein
Progress on the Subject of Immensity by Leslie Ullman
Losing the Ring in the River by Marge Saiser
Say That by Felecia Caton Garcia
City of Slow Dissolve by John Chávez
Breaths by Eleuterio Santiago-Díaz

For additional titles in the Mary Burritt Christiansen Poetry Series, please
visit unmpress.com.

Report *to the* Department *of the* Interior

poems

DIANE GLANCY

University of New Mexico Press • Albuquerque

© 2015 by Diane Glancy
All rights reserved. Published 2015
Printed in the United States of America
20 19 18 17 16 15   1 2 3 4 5 6

Library of Congress Cataloging-in-Publication Data

Glancy, Diane.
 [Poems. Selections]
 Report to the Department of the Interior : poems / Diane Glancy.
     pages ; cm. — (Mary Burritt Christiansen poetry series)
 ISBN 978-0-8263-5571-3 (pbk. : alk. paper) — ISBN 978-0-8263-5572-0 (electronic)
 I. Title.
 PS3557.L294A6 2015
 811'.54—dc23

                        2014023097

Cover illustration: Wohaw (Kiowa), Untitled (Fort Marion), ledger-book drawing, ca. 1875.
Courtesy of Missouri History Museum, St. Louis.
Author photo courtesy of Christopher Grisanti
Book design by Catherine Leonardo
Composed in Minion Pro

If I beheld the sun when it shined

—Job 31:26

Contents

REPORT TO THE DEPARTMENT
OF THE INTERIOR

———∞∞∞———

A scene of raw despair—Indians sleeping on a filthy floor.
A man who sobbed at night and tried to articulate the reason.

— Richard Hugo, "Letter to [James] Welch from
Browning [Montana]"

Postscript at the Beginning

History is the hard part of the story. Let Indian education and first government–contact speak. Early missionaries, evangelists, government agents, educationists, boarding schoolists, Sunday schoolists. Winter after winter they crowded the sidewalk to school. Shivering. Shivering. The clouds lined up in their school rows. Not another sad-sack story of assimilation. But with respect to relatives—we have arrived on the other side of learning. The history of these voices walks with us.

Report (1)

Hide me in your quiver

       —Isaiah 49:2

It moved inside us,
the old story before the story,
a remembrance of memory,
a fleeing too hard to forget.

In the primitive landscape
bushes became wolves
and the wolves wrote the government reports.
They strung our hunting grounds with their words,
leaving a trail we followed.

Once our stories were round
but the wolves made them square as houses.

Bite off the corners of their books
until they are round as pie plates
on the counter in the crowded café.

The wolves kept up their reports—
betrayal—
betrayal—
on the shelving and window sash.
Their reportage only made what happened
happen again on paper,
a map-work still legible as rock drawings.

I tell you they occupied the land
leaving us to this day
their bookshelves and cabinetry.

BULL HEAD'S WIFE

———∞∞∞———

The Indian felt . . . very Indian all those shots flying . . .
who knew they were turning into the gunnery-sergeant's
field report . . . all not totally fallen but nearly . . .
between the shots flying there.

Bull Head's Wife on the Eighty-Mile Journey to Her Wounded Husband Who Had Just Killed Sitting Bull

They didn't do it themselves. They got us to do it.
They divided us—it was us against ourselves.
My husband, the lieutenant of police,
led the group to Sitting Bull, the *hostile*.
I was away.
My family had called me to their camp
on Cannonball River.
I saw the runner.
I knew it was about Bull Head.
I knew my husband was in trouble.
But shot?
Near death?
I started immediately.

The runner already was far ahead.
A coyote who went with me said nothing.
I followed an old trail.
Twenty miles a day, I suppose.
I slept once in the leaves in a ravine.
The clumps of grass rattled their stories.
I dug roots.
I ate dried buffalo meat that my sister
wrapped in a medicine pouch.
I heard my mother's voice.
She spoke my tiredness out of the way.
The coyote was my father's voice
saying nothing I could hear.

I heard the birds.
They said, *go, go, go.*
They were chirping.
The leaves were howling.
The wind was an uncle

who said Bull Head would be dead soon.
I had to see him.
I had to tell him he'd been a good husband.
He had to know that for his trip through the stars.

We'd betrayed our own people.
He'd know that soon.
It was something I didn't tell him.
We had our different ways to see.
I ran until my feet were torn and bruised.
I ran eighty miles.

Fort Yates' Infirmary: Bull Head's Wife Falls in a Faint
     at His Bed

Berry berry I am your berry—the berries of your eyes—
the white berries of your teeth—the berries at the joints of your fingers—
the berries of your knucklebones—these berries—
these small burial mounds.

His thigh soaked in bloody rags.
Doesn't anything they do work?
There are wrappings and changings.
He moans at every turn.
I hear the wind in his breath.
A pine tree grows from his head.
The spirits wait at the end of his bed.
The elders shake their medicine rattle for his healing.
He talks to the voices from the other world.
The spirits don't leave.
They hold a buffalo robe over their arm to wrap him for the journey.
I hit them when he isn't looking.
I stomp on their feet.
I smell the sour wind.

Postscript:
The wheelbarrow shell without handles and wheels
upside-down in the yard
is the turtle-shell rattle they shook for him.

Military Honors at Fort Yates, North Dakota, December 20, 1890

I stood with his father and brother at the head of his grave.
Bull Head, lieutenant of the Indian police,
went to Sitting Bull's house with a warrant for his arrest.
Hostiles, they were called.
Bull Head shot Sitting Bull in the heart.
Sitting Bull shot Bull Head in the thigh as he fell.
How could the wound kill him there?

Postscript:
Among Sitting Bull's belongings were letters
from Mrs. Weldon of New York
warning him to leave the agency
because the government was planning to kill him:
Flee the agency flee they will kill you
they will hit you with bullets
the impastoned are here
carrying their pallet knives
they will take your moccasins
and clothes for relics
they will scalp
they will saw each hair from your head.

When Cézanne Visited America and Made These Little
    Dialogues
These Little Strokes of Brush for Bibemus Quarry at Pipestone

To paint landscape, I need to know the structure of the land.

—Paul Cézanne

I take your pallet knife
lick with my tongue
the yellows I taste
the reds I swallow
the broad blunt brush of blue
for shadows in the crevices of quarry.

Postscript (1):
You've seen those shadows there
where the highway cuts through a hill.
Both sides rising on each side—
where the road is a slit in the toaster.

Postscript (2):
Cézanne was never in America.

Comment:
He was in the world of this book.

Wolf Dreaming

I cut my arm with a kitchen knife after Bull Head's death.
In his aftermath, he left a pine.
Long ago, I watched him before he knew I would be his wife.
He was made a lieutenant in the U.S. military police.
His horse had metal shoes.

Now I see his trail through the sky.
We will walk where the stars are cacti
picking our memories like thorns:
the bullet you sent into Sitting Bull—his fire in your thigh.

Postscript:
Bull Head's death was tearing off a fingernail.
When the finger heals there is a scar
like the image of a moon where the nail had been.

What voice is that?
Bull Head?
I go on without him
calling his name.

The Spirit of Bull Head's Wife Visits the National Gallery of Art,
    Washington, D.C., and Views *The Artist's Father, Reading
    "L'Evenement,"* Paul Cézanne

I saw a man with pages standing up on his arms and chest
as if he were wearing the pages
as if pages were his whole being—
step near the campfire, dear,
let me see you flame.

How far apart
yet overlaid with sameness that is somehow an elastic waist
too tight
the blur of stories—

Lieut. Henry Bull Head with 39 of his men and a few volunteers
entered Sitting Bull's camp December 16th
Bull Head
1st Sergt. Shave Head
2nd Sergt. Red Tomahawk
seven others entered Sitting Bull's house.
He started to dress for the journey but his son berated him
for going.
When the police took Sitting Bull from his house
they were surrounded by Sitting Bull's camp.
Sitting Bull told his men if they killed Bull Head and his officers
the others would run.
Catch the Bear and Strike the Kettle fired first
hitting Bull Head who shot Sitting Bull as he fell.
It was 43 policemen and volunteers against 150
of Sitting Bull's men.

That betrayal—
as if Bull Head was a *traitor* of his people.
No—it was the dilemma of a man
reading the *Event* on the wind
and seeing a trail of smoke in the distance
become the pages he read.

Bull Head's Wife Opens Ristorante Hortense Fiquet, Fort Yates, North Dakota

Warm beet tart with chevre   6
Spinach, Bull Head blue cheese, balsamic vinaigrette   7
Pan-roasted prairie rainbow trout wrapped in ham   22
Oven-roasted pheasant with creamy horseradish-ramp risotto   24
Grilled leg of elk with yellow-potato puree, grilled baby artichoke, and
    dried cherries   26
Braised pheasant with roasted leek and pheasant eggs   27
Catch of the day   Market price

Bull Head's Wife Studies Frances Glessner Lee's Visible Proofs,
   A Series of Crime Scenes Reconstructed in Miniature in the
   1940s and '50s for Use in Forensics

Henry Bull Head, First Lieutenant of Police, died 82 hours after the fight
Charles Shave Head, First Sergeant of Police, died 25 hours after the fight
James Little Eagle, Fourth Sergeant of Police, killed in the fight
Paul Afraid-of-Soldiers, Private of Police, killed in the fight
John Armstrong, Special Police, killed in the fight
David Hawkman, Special Police, killed in the fight
Alexander Middle, Private of Police, wounded, recovering
Sitting Bull, killed, 56 years of age
Crow Foot (Sitting Bull's son), killed, 17 years of age
Black Bird, killed, 43 years of age
Catch the Bear, killed, 44 years of age
Spotted Horn Bull, killed, 56 years of age
Brave Thunder, No. 1, killed, 46 years of age
Little Assiniboine, killed, 44 years of age
Chase Wounded, killed, 24 years of age
Bull Ghost, wounded, entirely recovered
Brave Thunder, No. 2, wounded, recovering rapidly
Strike the Kettle, wounded, now at Fort Sully, a prisoner

Postscript:
+ wives and children who depended upon them

Nutshell Studies of Unexplained Death: Bull Head's Wife Reconstructs a Miniature of Sitting Bull's Camp

The division commander directed Bull Head to secure Sitting Bull—
Acknowledge receipt and if not clear report back.
(Signed) M. Barber, Assistant Adjutant General.

This is the time many of the Indians are gone to the fort for biweekly rations—
James McLaughlin, Indian Agent, advised by telegraph for suppression
of the outbreak among Sioux Indians

I make the land flat.
I make the houses and surrounding teepees.
I make Bull Head's badge of military police.
I make the bullets—

I take my husband on a mission
to arrest Sitting Bull who defied the government,
who was stuck on the Messianic craze,
who resisted—

I make betrayal.
I make grief.
I make spirit lines for firearms
marking the flight of the bullet to Bull Head's thigh.
I post little flags at the crime scene—

Postscript:
A muffler with its tail pipe curled by the road like a snake still tells
the story.

Bull Head's Wife Mail-Orders at the Telegraph Office

I am cold Stop I am cold Stop I am thrashing with cold Stop Send a
blanket Stop Cover me with a buffalo robe Stop The river is a knife Stop
My horse is shivering Stop I have frost for hair Stop The snow geese are
calling Stop Their cries are the north wind Stop I hear them say *frio frio
blanco blanco* Stop The air is full of birds Stop I am the only tree on the
prairie Stop My teeth are ice Stop The cries of the foxes are a white
pickup Stop *Hey yanno* Stop Send galoshes for the buffalo Stop Send
parka Stop Send snowshoes Stop The clouds cover the land with snow
Stop The wind is copied double-sided Stop

Bull Head's Wife Reads Cliff Notes
of Indian History

The spider
made
herself
thin
as a
needle
sat
quietly
invisibly
still-ly
waiting
for
the gnats
to catch
her web
in a corner
of the
window
squid-like
minute
decimal
if squids
were
the size
of
an insect.

SPOTTED TAIL'S DAUGHTER [1848–1866]

———⚬⚬⚬———

Long trains of wagons winding their way over the plains.
The mysterious telegraph wires stretching across their
hunting grounds to the mountains, engineers surveying
a route for a track for the iron horse . . .

—Sergeant Stephen Fairfield, 11th Kansas Cavalry, 1865

Spotted Tail's Daughter [1848–1866]

I look down on the prairie
the way satellites track movement on the land.

I am Ah-ho-ap-pa, Wheat Flour
or Hinzinwin, Yellow Girl,
or Yellow Buckskin Girl
or Girl that Owned the Yellow Mare
or Yellow Leaf
or Falling Leaf
or Mini-aku, Brings Water.

I was Spotted Tail's favorite daughter.
After my death, he lost the heart to fight.

I was with him when he killed Lieutenant Grattan
and his men [1854]
and fought at the Battle of Blue Water Creek
against Brevet Brig. General William Harney's forces [1855].
I was with him at all the skirmishes.

I lived at Fort Laramie [1855–1856] when my father was in prison.
I often visited the houses of officers' wives.

General Harney gave me a red Episcopal prayer book
with a cross on it.
I held it in my hand.
Spirits seemed to fly from it, rising and landing again.
I think now it was an airfield.

My father was through attacking mail wagons
and U.S. troops.
There was nothing left he could do.
Our game was gone.

Our land was lined with wagon wheels.
Soon there would be rails.

The soldiers made Spotted Tail and his men
sign a treaty to protect the new road through the country.
Their X marked the Treaty at Fort Laramie:
Spotted Tail, Brule Ring Band, and head chief of the Brules
Swift Bear, Brule Corn Band
Dog Hawk, Brule Orphan Band
Hawk Thunder, Brule
Standing Elk, Brule Corn Band
Tall Mandan, Brule soldier
Brave Heart, Brule chief.

I don't know why I died.
When I returned to our camp,
I coughed until my sides hurt
and didn't want to cough again.
We had nothing but horsehide to chew,
the icy wind to drink.
A runner went from our camp to Fort Laramie
to tell Colonel Maynadier I was sick.
He sent an ambulance
with an escort of one company of cavalry
and two howitzers
to bring us to the fort.

I asked to be buried at Fort Laramie
where Chief Smoke had been buried.
He was a stay-by-the-fort,
an Indian who gave up the fight early
and waited for rations.

I was wrapped in buffalo robes and bound with cords.
I was laid in a pine coffin
and received the funeral offerings.

Colonel Maynadier placed gauntlets in the coffin
so I could keep my hands warm.
Other officers gave moccasins,
red flannel, and clothes to wear on my way
to the spirit world.
The Indians gave me an embroidered pinecone,
a small mirror, and strings of beads.
Each whispered something to me.
I didn't like you.
I wanted to be Spotted Tail's favorite daughter.
You are going where there is plenty of game and no snowstorms.
Take me with you—
The wind has pushed upriver in my heart.

Spotted Tail gave my red prayer book to Rev. Alpha Wright—
it was the book General Harney gave me.
The reverend placed it inside my coffin
when he finished my service.
My coffin was nailed shut,
covered with a red cloth and placed on a gun carriage
followed by relatives and officers.
Behind me a throng of troops and Indians.
I sat at the guard post and watched.

My coffin was lifted on the scaffold at sunset
to keep my body away from wolves and other animals.
The sun would bring the light again—
Those were the last words I heard from the earth.
My scaffold was near old Chief Smoke.
My head toward the east.

The Indians killed two ponies,
cut off the tails and heads,
attached the heads to the two forward posts of the scaffold,
the tails to the rear posts.
I would ride to the spirit land on the ponies.

That first bitter night,
I heard the wind that hummed along the telegraph wire.
I heard the watch-guard's cough in the cold,
the loneliness of my father,
the sound of wolves
knowing they could not reach my body.

I mounted a pony and led the other with a rope.
Water for the animals froze on our way to the spirit land.

Later [1875] the scaffold and coffin
were in danger of collapse.
Theodore Brown, a hospital steward,
removed the scaffold and buried my bones in the ground.

A year later, Spotted Tail came
to take my remains back to the Rosebud Agency
for permanent burial.
I didn't want to go—
We had traded at Fort Laramie.
The soldiers raced their horses,
and the great Father's people had been good to us.
Now all of that had passed
and Spotted Tail wanted our dead in one place.
He came to take my bones to the Rosebud Agency
on Beaver Creek.

The soldiers dug for my bones,
but my father didn't get all of them.
Maybe by chance he left a part there—
like the small streaks of falling stars.
I am buried at Fort Laramie and the Rosebud Reservation.
I have two graves.

At night I throw a bead from my funeral offerings
trying to hit the earth.

ONE CALL AWAY

⟨⟩

The Office of Indian Affairs was established March 11, 1824
as part of the United States Department of War.
In 1847, the Office was renamed the Bureau of Indian Affairs.
In 1849, the Bureau was moved to the Department of the Interior
because Indian affairs now focused on what to do with land
that had been inhabited by the Indians.
Soon after, reformers and missionaries began the slow attempt
to assimilate and evangelize the different tribes
whose land it had been.

Indian education began in prison
in boarding school
in upheaval
in defeat.
It was one call away from death.

The Book

It sat on the table
silent as a rabbit.
We could not leave the room.
We had to stay there with it.
We were inhabitants of their promised land.
The ears long as clouds.
The paws the rampage of waves.

Postscript:
In 1875, after the last of the Plains Indians Wars,
Lieutenant Richard Henry Pratt took seventy-two prisoners
from Indian Territory [later Oklahoma]
to Fort Marion in St. Augustine, Florida,
where he began educating the prisoners.
Afterward there followed a proliferation of reservation
and boarding schools including Carlisle Indian
Industrial School in Pennsylvania established by Pratt.

To Say from Their Way

The schools were soon up
and required overseeings of the upmost kind
to acquire competence and meet expectations.

Whatever they said
was said in government reports
and filed in drawers that might be read again.

But schools cannot be contained on pages.
Dear Sir, if only you were here
you would know the conditions.

A forest of closed doors
behind which there is a breaking into people
with a world not theirs.

Reports (2)

Report from Ouray Agency Boarding School, July 1, 1898
Miss Estelle Reel, Superintendent of Indian Schools
The attendance has been very small throughout the year. These Indians are still bitterly and unreasonably opposed to education. When asked to give their children a chance to learn something, they always have excuses ready.
I am, respectfully yours, H. J. Curtis

Truant report: reason for opposition, July 1, 1898
We sat on hard wooden benches in the classroom.
We ate at long tables.
They stood over us when we went outside.
We slept in a room with rows of beds.
The room was locked at night.
We were counted every morning.
They never turned their heads.
Respectfully yours, Nathan Moving Bear

Annual Report of the Department of the Interior, for the Fiscal Year
Ended June 30, 1898, Indian Affairs, Washington, D.C.
Report of Red Lake Agency, Minnesota
Eight schools in bad repair are located in this agency, 7 boarding schools and 1 day school, the average attendance being 442. If better school buildings are erected, more pupils could be accommodated. Congress has appropriated funds for the erection of school buildings at Red Lake and Leech Lake. Both places are badly in need of new buildings, although the superintendents of the schools have kept up the attendance to the capacity of the present buildings.
John H. Sutherland, United States Indian Agent

Truant report: reason for opposition
We were expected to learn something unrelated

to anything we understood. We would have to learn the structure
before we learned the meaning the structure held.

But the structure was not explained.

[No name attached to this report.]

Those Old Voices Always Are with Me

If they could have taught velocity as an arrow shot at a buffalo running
multi-directionally in varying prairie winds from a moving horse—

If they could have said 1 buffalo + 0 buffalo is still 1 buffalo—

If they could have said all would disappear, yet return in different form,
and we just had to recognize the variables of its transformation—

If they could have said that time-space was visiting relatives a three-day
journey away by train as we lay in our beds in boarding school—

If they had just said how it takes more than one name to name a person—

If they could have said the marks of their numbers on the blackboard
explained the changing force of a vision quest—

If they could have explained thermodynamics as our visions during a
sun dance—

If they would have said the black hole was a boarding school.

Report on Indian Education from the Indian

Pis'kun [buffalo jump]
Head-Smashed-in-Buffalo-Jump, near Fort Macleod, Alberta

Before the horse and gun, buffalo were hunted on foot.
There was a long time learning how to do this.
It did not come in a school year.
There were no classrooms. No square books.

For a long time the Indians studied the herds of buffalo
and the packs of wolves that hunted them.
They saw how the buffalo gathered around their young.
Nothing was more important than the calves.
If one was in distress, the buffalo went to it.

The Indians saw that the wolves came in groups to the weakest calf
and waited until its mother was eating grass.

Off the northern slopes of the Rockies
the strong winds stampede the prairie grass.
The Indians watched from the cliff—
if the buffalo would run like the grass
they could not stop.
The buffalo would fall over the cliff.
They would die.

In a time of hunger, a woman gathering twigs heard a voice.
It was a rock shaped like a buffalo.
In the night, she dreamed a buffalo song
that would call the buffalo to a gathering place near the cliff.
She told the elders who began to think
how the killing could be done.

Iniskim was the name of the sacred buffalo stone.

In the fall when the leaves were yellow
and the buffalo fat from eating summer grass,
Indians prepared a drive lane to the cliff,
dragging a buffalo hide across the grasses
so the buffalo would smell their own kind as they ran.

The Indians gathered rocks and branches to narrow the lane
toward the cliff.

For a ceremony, the woman sang the buffalo song
she dreamed in a night of hunger.

Several boys wearing wolfskin
crawled to the back of the herd.
The buffalo saw the wolves
and became skittish as they grazed.

Another boy in buffalo skin
crawled past the buffalo toward the cliff.
He cried like a calf.
The herd moved toward it.
The Indians waved branches and yelled.
The boy turned out of the way.
The skittish buffalo panicked and ran
thundering over the cliff.

The buffalo that survived
would warn others not to panic and run.
With grooved hammerstones
the Indians smashed the heads
of any buffalo still alive.

Truant Reports: Reason for Opposition

Indian education, to the Indian, has to do with relationship to The Maker,
to community, to land and animals.
It pointed outward to others.
How to become a whole person.
Everything belonged to the Spirit.
Integration of self into alignment with other elements
gave a sense of purpose and a way of *being* in the world.
Indian boarding schools tried to erase the Indian from the Indian
and make him someone else
without consideration of his structure of learning, his language or
culture.
Educators worked in vain to stamp out Indian culture
that was denounced as the source of Indian poverty.
Indian schools were replicas of white schools and were relatively
meaningless to the Indian.

One Call Away

This is not my world—
a buffalo jump
a dissolution.
I went in one person and came out another.
I learned apathy—in boarding school I learned to drag my feet—
school—where the next world is one call away.

A Voice from Another Room—Report from the Cherokee Female Seminary, Tahlequah, Oklahoma, Founded 1851

I had my own bed with others in a row.
I had food to eat.
I had a place away from those that came and went at night.
And yelled and fought and threatened to burn the house.
I was where no one would hurt.
I knew what to do and when.

5:30 a.m. Students Rise
6:00–7:00 a.m. Study Hall
7:00–8:30 a.m. Breakfast and Detail
8:30–9:00 a.m. Chapel
9:00 a.m.–12:00 p.m. Recitations
12:00–2:00 p.m. Noon Break
2:00–4:00 p.m. Recitations
4:15–4:45 p.m. Exercises
5:00 p.m. Dinner
6:45–8:45 p.m. Study Hall
9:00 p.m. First Retiring Bell
9:15 p.m. Second Retiring Bell

We studied Latin
Math
Science
Rhetoric
Composition
Geography
Philosophy
Religion.
There were music recitals.
We published our own newspaper—*Cherokee Rose Buds.*

We held council.
They heard our voices.
I was hall monitor.
They knew we were there.

Cliff Notes from Frances Willard Grade School, 1948

I slept to the waking that sleep was supposed to wake to.
The darkness of sleep let me know I was in darkness.
Dark. Dark. Wake from it. Wake.
It's the cold mornings I remember.
I walked up the hill to school.
I sat stiff in the metal chair all day without moving.
I walked down the hill from school.
I am nothing.
I am nothing.
Those were the lessons I carried in my satchel.
I sat in back of the room.
Outside the world industrialized.
Utilitarian.

Too Hard to Forget

Indian education, it seems to me, has been a lesson in *reductionism*, in living as a stranger to self. Living without part of oneself. Living outside oneself. Living with a smaller self. Often, the Indian was not able to return to tribal life, or able to make a living in the new world. Yet, I must say that education has been the key to my life. I hardly can speak of it without the old lump closing off my throat. Memories of isolation, of being pushed to the back row, of staying there by choice, of terror, loneliness, silence, low grades. Yet I finally got through in the shape of the stranger I am.

What Shape Did You Take?
Indian Boarding School, Morris, Minnesota, 1902

What did you do when the cold wind blew
through those rooms? What shape did you take
when your teeth were ice? What did you do
when your brothers ran away from school
and were brought back and whipped
in front of the class? Did you remember
their ponies lapping Ottertail Creek
when you heard the lashes? How did you twist
your mind to bear up? What did you hear
the boarding school say? Did the walls cry out
to the dark of each cold night? What did you do
when the sun fell crooked in the sky
and the moon rolled flat along the horizon?
What did you do when the stars seized in the darkness?
What did you answer when the comets asked you
to come with them on their travois?
What did you do when your bare feet touched the floor
and you pulled off your thin nightshirt
and dressed in the cold?—your bones spiky
as the skeleton of a sea horse, and from as far away.
What did you do those nights your stomach growled
for buffalo meat and prairie turnips—
and your days sank as if trying to stampede under
creek water when the world clattered and drowned?
What did you do when the wolves spelled
your new name and looked at you
from the little black Bibles of their eyes?
What did you say to the ghosts of your brothers
that haunted the boarding school?
Did you remember the black quarter moons of dirt
under their fingernails from field work?

Did you dream of the sound of their feet shattering
the thin ice sheet on the creek as they tried
to run again?—Do you still hear the hooves
of the horses after them?

Each Day Pulls like a Hill to Climb

Sometimes I wake with something in my throat.
What can I say now—washed of all that was?—
It is here I stand beside my washing machine
with this Maker and his redeemer man.

SQUEEZING THROUGH THE NARROW
DOOR OF THE BOARDING SCHOOL

———⚬⚬⚬———

Carlisle Indian Industrial School, established by Richard Henry
Pratt, Carlisle, Pennsylvania [1879–1918]

Lo, the poor Indian! whose untutored mind
Sees God in clouds, or hears him in the wind—

—Alexander Pope, *An Essay on Man*

First Train from North Dakota to Carlisle Indian Industrial School in Eastern Pennsylvania

We had been wrapped in a fox robe.
We had worn buffalo hide.
Now we rode the train for several days.
We whimpered. We cried.
Where was this new world?
Why had our parents sent us away?
The passing land was a blur when we looked from the train.
We arrived in the middle of the night.
There was no food, no beds, bedding, nothing.
We slept on a cold floor.
Later, we would say there was nothing shining.
We were confined to our beds before dark
without stories.
That was the hardest part—no voices telling stories.
We tried to make up our own stories:
All the deer went away.
The fox. The buffalo. The wild turkey.
When we got to nothing we would build the story again.
We knew a story could rise as wind in the night.
Maybe stories traveled overland.
Maybe stories rode the train.
If we didn't hear the stories, we could die.
It already had happened, not the coughing disease,
but the willful dying.

The Indian Education Problem Always Has Been There

The school was a paper house with edges that cut.
We soon morphed into strange beings with short hair and trousers.
What was that cawing in the dark
with everyone asleep / dreaming in the old hunting grounds?
The buffalo snorted at our ears.
The trees lost their leaves across the school grounds at Carlisle.
Whatever we did would turn to leaves and fall.
The school where we could sit forever in chairs
and not know what they meant.

It Was Enough They Came and Got Us

It was enough they came and got us—and took us to boarding schools.
It was worse when our parents sent us—disoriented, shaken, confused.
You know it in the cemetery at Carlisle Indian Industrial School—

Some of the names:
Launy Shorty, Piegan
Joan Lumpfoot, Arapahoe
Jemima John, Oneida
Tomicock, Eskimo
Joan Louisa, Pima
Owen Fiery
Titus Deerhead
Zeneke Uh
Thomas Marshall, age 19 of measles
Twelve graves marked, Unknown

From the beginning, education was lethal.

Reveille

Drill
Make beds
Breakfast
Assembly and roll call
Care of teeth
Inspection
School
Assembly and roll call
Dinner
Pupils at liberty
Industrial call for work
Gymnasium classes
Supper
Assembly and roll call
Care of teeth
Recreation
Roll call and inspection
Call to quarters to prepare lessons
Pupils retire
Bed check and taps
On Sundays, church attendance in town

No More Stories Told by the Voice

Now it was penmanship covering our voices
with the sound of handwriting—
awkward marks on the slate boards—
chalk squeaking like the turn of a wagon hitch
or a hinged door.
In our writing we heard the sound of an animal scratching
under our barracks—
It was the beginning of writing—
the looking into—the hearing-what-else-is-there.

In the night the sky wailed like a train whistle
that brought us from the prairie.
We slept as if awake.

The crows were crying for the sacred sound of meaning.
They held out their stark wings—
We pulled their crow feathers over our arms—
our dreams were visions of land passing beneath us
back to our reservation—
past fences strung as ruled tablets—
or the journey to The Maker in another world
where we could migrate across the land again.
The crows were noisy—they were noisy—
In their beaks, the song that stole us away.

We felt The Maker's arms between the earth and the sky above us.
When we were in the air we saw the ancestors
as though they would drop from the stars.
Take the writing lessons, they said,
the loop of planets—the straight-line comets are slates
that carry our words.

Reports (3)

Dennis Thomas shuffles, slouches, sprawls his legs in the aisle, no socks,
thinly clad on cold days to get attention, in general a nuisance—

Abraham Hill crushed his right arm and two fingers trying to jump the
train.

Cecelia Matlock—large—slow—complains all day of hot summer
months in the laundry—

Charles Packineau's mangled body was found by the railroad tracks by
his brother, David, who escorted his body back to Elbowoods, ND.

The Train Tracks

The railroad tracks ran beside
the Carlisle Indian Industrial School—
the tracks were of themselves nothing resting on crossties.
They were for the train wheels grooved to roll
along the rails.
It takes two of them, helpless, standing side by side—
like grandparents behind the train
when it pulled away.
The tracks shone in the moonlight.
They spoke before a train arrived.
The iron for the tracks was brought from underground—
melted and shaped as we were shaped—
our skinny spines lying side by side—stiff—unmoving—
to transport ourselves away.

School

The stall of a single ox is four feet wide; and since the animals are usually stalled four abreast, just as they had been yoked to the plough, how many feet is one division of the ox house?

What did we know of an ox house? What did we know of plough?

Course work was unrelated to our lives.
The boarding school was overcrowded.
There wasn't enough to eat.
Discipline was strict / severe.
Sick children were not treated, which led to frequent epidemics
of tuberculosis and trachoma.
We worked long hours in shops, fields, kitchens, laundries, leather shops.

There were two world views that could not coexist.

The verbs were hardest—to see them conjugated—formed in stalls.

What stallage was this?
No one baiting whatever could be hooked.
It was stall-work.
This school.
This abiding school.

In Winter the Storm Wind Rattles the Weather Stripping of the
Door like a Train in the Distance

My legs are railroad tracks.
My heart chugs in my chest.
I am traveling with these old reports.
This bundle of voices in my throat.

THE VISIONS OF FATHER PHILIP BERNARD

————✦✦✦————

Holy Redeemer Boarding School, Quanah, Texas, 1947

Postscript (1):
The boarding school is fictional. Quanah, Texas, is not.

The Visions of Father Philip Bernard

Does not God cleanse his sanctuary?
We establish you, O Lord.

Give Abraham Bull five lashes behind each knee.
Isn't it better than Hell?

For Solomon's offense, take his blanket.
For Ezekiel's offense, take the sheet from his bed.
Let the wool blanket chaff his skin.
I see the flakes and red patches.
What is it that eats his skin?

I had hoped for more.
Not an insignificant outpost.
Not this small room lit by a wood stove too hot in the center.
Too cold in the corner of the room
where I push my bed away from the scorching heat.

Nevertheless I kneel in prayer, O Lord, to you.

Who is it—in the corner of the ceiling?
I would think it was an angel,
but it wears a buffalo head with horns for a hat.
I don't want to stare, but it is frightful.

When did I offend you, God, that I suffer here?
Who was against me that I was sent to an outpost?

Days on the train from the east.
I never have seen any place this barren.
The flat land under the flat sky.
A few trees bent to the north by the wind.
I stood frozen on the steps.

The conductor insisted I get off. They had a schedule to keep.
I think it was his hand on my back.
Otherwise, I could not have descended to the platform.
Was it Brother Fornace who met me?

Blessed is your rod and repeating rifle.
The ages to come are with me.
Yet the sky blooms with dawn after darkness.

Henry Toes continues to bellow.
For his offense, offer no comfort.
Let the boys tease him for his noise.
Turn them against one another. Confound their ways.
It will last into the coming generations.

What horses are running?

I get these tail winds. These head winds in my throat.
The Lord speaks with his mighty voice.
The spirit with the buffalo head speaks also.

I hear it though I don't listen.

The dawn is a water moccasin.
The clouds are sinewy in the sky.

Sister Cornice Pavel. Sister Patience!
Keep them separate—the boys from the girls.
We don't want more of them.

What are these visions?
Who is the author of them?—

The spirit wearing a buffalo head comes to visit.
It is insistent.
You brought your sickness and offered your medicine.

Holy stalk.
Redeemer and judge.
Am I to witness these accusations?
Am I the recipient of a spirit's words?

My judge is the living God.
My judgment is the harsh winter on the high plains.
Yet the sun coming open on clear mornings offers
its campfire.

We don't think you should be here.
Did you ask permission?

Would you have given it?

God of the Church. God of the boarding school.
We come to you, O Lord, to learn.
Wake us from our sleep.
We flinch in the glare of the sun against the window glass.
God of the cross. The evening grass. The turnip fields.

They slept on the ground. I gave them a cot.
They were hungry. I gave them bread.
They were purposeless. I gave them a ruler.
A pencil. A tablet.
They wandered on the prairie.
I gave them a schedule to follow.
I divided their days into compartments.
I offered them order.

Sister Cornice Pavel's skin is chapped nearly raw.
I can hardly look at her.
Should she be quarantined with Ezekiel,
who scratches the sores from his wool blanket?

Sister Patience is runny-eyed.
Brother Fornace stirs the frozen mud with his rake.

He makes little furrows in the snow.
What are you planting? Snowflakes?

What do we do with the earaches?
The sore throats?
The whimperings and whinings?

Horace Freely's temperature is boiling.
There will be another grave in the cemetery.

For Lester Bear's offense
give three hard raps to the back of his head.

Shame Sarah Blackhawk in front of others.
She can hardly speak.
It will lock her in that place forever.

Hiram Blackbear stutters.
Make him speak in front of the class
until he knows there will be no respite from his puddling.

Let them be ashamed
and brought in confusion together—Psalm 35:26
I am grateful, Lord, for the guidance of your word.

Lord of Joy. Where is laughter?
Have I caused it to go?
At one time, in seminary, I could ignite a table in spasms
until I, too, was in trouble.

Some of the Indians will keep their ways.
No amount of punishment will drive it from them.
I can see it in the folds of their character,
though I unfold day and night.
Will I always find more folds?
Is there no end to them?

But for those I reach and change—
after I am through with them,
they will not be able to go back.
They won't be accepted as us, of course.
They will be strangers to both worlds.

You taught them bitterness and hurt—
the spirit wearing the buffalo head speaks.

I taught them God—I tell the spirit.

You make us strangers and sojourners
in a place we would not choose to be.

I believe it is our place now.

Do you see the small hill pointed at the top?
Do you see the mounds? The rises in the land?
They are the spirit of our people. Our voices are theirs.

You are willfully disobedient to the living God.
You are ignorant of his ways.
My purpose is to instill knowledge of God
at the Holy Redeemer Boarding School.
Or at least as much of a vision of him
as I can bring to this ungodly place.
These stiff-necked people.

I thought I was coming to a different climate.
Brother Fornace tells me the cold spell is unusual.
I feel more dampness.
It will snow again. More cold. More cracked lips.
More shivering. More harshness. More sickness.
Brother Fornace digs the graves.
Sister Patience weeps.
She feels sorry for every varmint,
vermin, and coyote we hear at night.

Make Cecil stand barefoot in the snow.
Let Randolph howl with a toothache. Do not pull.
Beat Rufus Fox on the soles of his feet.
Thereafter he will crawl.

Make them hateful to one another so they will see the Lord.

Quiet the hiss of the prairie wind.
Let them all be silent.

[Father Philip Bernard pauses a moment in silent prayer.]

I want to save them from hellfire.
Their dreadful sweat lodge is a foretaste of Hell.
What does the spirit know in its buffalo hat?
The sweat lodge is a purification ceremony—the spirit says.
I tell it no one can purify but Christ our Lord.

How can two holy men see different ways?

You are not a holy man—I hear the spirit say.
Nor are you, I answer.

I would take this place down brick by brick.
I see migrating birds as the bricks flying away.
They make a long and single line snaking through the sky.

If you were in our school.
If you were in ours.
I would not see your God.
Then you will be left out of his kingdom
to roast in the fire pit of Hell.

Claude Gray Bear arrives at the school with fleas.
Or lice. Soon everyone will be scratching.
Wash them in lye with a stiff brush.
Don't they know it is for their own good?

God, I hear the screeching.
Sister Cornice Pavel's arms are red to the elbows.
She cries at night as Sister Patience uses the ointment.
Play the organ.
The pitiful squeaking box out of sorts
after its trip across the prairie.

Who is there now? Brother Fornace?
Buford Sander has run away from school.
He is returned.
Thereafter hobbled.
Now Buford's eyes are red and swollen.
Some mornings they are crusted shut.
The blacksmith in Quanah visits
the Holy Redeemer Boarding School
to repair the lock on the front gate.

I ask the Holy Spirit to keep the others from truancy.

They have visions of a Maker.
That's what they call him—*Maker.*
But their Maker is not our Maker.
Subdue the land is your commandment, Lord God.
You, God, set up the Promised Lands
and told your people to enter
and ravage the ones who live there.
It is your scripture, God.
We obey your commandments.
Cast down everything that is not you.

We don't want to change. We want our lives.
Listen to me.
I don't want to listen to you.
I don't want to listen to you.

What torture does God have for me now?

At night, the quarter moon tries to bite the sky
with its open mouth.

Postscript (2):
The opening of the monologue came to me as I was driving before dawn,
11/28/13, near Quanah, Texas, on Highway 287 northwest toward
Amarillo to connect with I-40 back to California. Later, when I was
transferring my notes to my laptop, I looked up Quanah Parker online.
"The Quanah Parker Society, based in Cache, Oklahoma, holds an
annual family reunion and powwow. Events usually include a pilgrimage
to sacred sites in Quanah, Texas." It was in the early dawn of 11/28 that I
passed those sacred sites without knowing they were there. In the
crossroads of past and present, seen and unseen, near Quanah, Texas, on
Highway 287, eight miles south of the Red River that separates Texas and
Oklahoma, I picked up the voice of Father Philip Bernard.

THE SHOOTINGS AT RED LAKE RESERVATION

—⸺∽∽∽⸺—

The voices swam like fish in a tank,
each going their own way in the foreground and background
constantly moving.
Then I knew there was another fish tank behind the tank
I was watching.

The Shootings at Red Lake Reservation, Red Lake, Minnesota,
   March 21, 2005

It was the dreams. They came like arrows.
Sometimes I woke remembering something long ago.
Other times I knew I only dreamed.
Sometimes I heard the hiss of an arrow hitting its
mark—SCHWUUUUUUUUPP!!
It was something I wanted to hear again.
I slept hoping I would dream.

It was the aquarium light I watched at school.
I think the fish called to me there.

The dreams hid when the nightmares came.
The fish sat on the bed. He said not to be afraid.
He asked if I was hungry. I opened my mouth.
I heard a car. My father came in.
He sobbed in his bed. He slept.
I woke in the morning crying.
Shut up, my father says.
He has worries—He has things that take him from me—
My father was defeated.
He killed himself—Shot himself in the head.

There was a fish inside me growling.

I cried but she did not hear—
My mother's mouth moved—
She slept with her large eye open on the side of her head.
Drunk. She swam on the highway. She slid off the road.
I was in the room. They were talking to me.
Someone would stay with me. They were outside talking.
No one heard the fish. I cried but they didn't hear.
My mother was in an accident—Driving while drunk.
Would she die?

There was blackness in the house.
The moving voices there.
Frogs. Snakes. Creeping things I felt around my ankles.
But a fish does not have ankles.
Then neither did I.

No one remembered I was there.
I looked for something to eat. There was nothing.
I felt the fish in my stomach and was not hungry.
If I could hunt, I would shoot a squirrel.
I would kill a fox. I would eat them whole.

Sometimes a river moves in me.
It is swimming with awful things.
My mother will not be home.
She doesn't know me. She is not herself.
She's a ghost. She has gone somewhere.
There is someone who looks like a mother. But she is not.
The fish knows it too. We talk about who she is.
We know it is not her. We look for my mother in the river.
The fish does not find her.

I was a bottom-feeder. Worst kind.
I was nothing. Had nothing. Anger choked me.
It caught my fin in its trap. The world was heavy.
It was bleeding. I was a throwaway.
I tried to find a footing, but always slipped back.
No one cared. Blast them.

I was stupid. I didn't know what they were doing.
They set up rules. I could never understand.
I could not do.

My mother never came back.
I heard those rodents in the walls of the house.
I knew when they slept on my bones.

Those rabbits I caught and poked a stick into—
Let them squirm. Let them know what it is to hurt.

The teachers said I was trouble. No one stood up for me.
Everyone said I was trouble. What would they do with me?

I went into the river. I lived with fish.
They would not find me there.

I visited my mother in the hospital in Minneapolis.
She was in her own hell.
The fish said my mother was sorry she was the way she was.
It was her spirit that left—It got up and went away,
and left her the way she was.

I wanted to shoot myself—I would take others with me—
The fish? More than the fish.
Everyone who left me in blackness.
I tried to swim away, but could not.
I was in the school's homebound program
for violation of school policy.
I posted messages on a neo-Nazi website.
Signed myself *Todesengel*, German for angel of death.
Wasn't it the Nazis who used the 7th Cavalry Indian extermination
    policy
you jerk and murdered Jews the same as the cavalry massacred Indians?
This cloudy logic. This murky underwater.
This taking on of enemy clothes.

Now the fish was in the aquarium light of the computer.
The screen glowed in the dark room.
My eyes moved online in REM sleep reading the screen.
I entered a river in which death could—what?
The nightmares hunted me.
I felt their teeth. I felt my eyes swim like a fish.

I planned a raid with my friends. We would blow them away—
Drive like warriors over the land. Our names would be known.
We would bring hell into this *dull*—
We would be legend. My eyes swam through our e-mails.

Where's the hook to pull the fish out?
There is none—None. I would kill the world.

It was purpose. It was buzz.
It was the hunt. They had taken our world placed theirs over ours
and said it was ours now too.

I do not want anyone guessing what this means.
We are underwater now. The hook is in our mouth.
We were connected by e-mail. It was power. It was grace.

The school put me out. I felt the warrior blood.
The urge to war—To prove myself a warrior fish.

The fish said I could kill.
The others wouldn't come with me.

It was cold—my grandmother's house where I lived.
The fish called me underwater.
His fins moved like waves on the screen.
The fish taught me to hold a rifle.
He said he did not have arms.
He was a fish and I could hold the rifle for him.

I went to my grandfather's house—Killed him and his girlfriend.
Took his shotgun and walked into school.

I blasted my way into Red Lake High School
past the metal detector. Killed the security guard.
Killed a teacher, students, wounded others
with two handguns and my grandfather's shotgun.

I blew them away—They didn't know I was coming.
They weren't looking for a fish—

The water in the aquarium parted and I passed through.

I shot myself or someone did in the shootout.
No, I shot myself after I had been shot.

A fish swells with rage.
A fish grows arms.
A fish lurches forward.
A fish holds a gun.

REPORT (4)

⸻

On the road I picked up a bird's nest.
On the road I picked up a rock like the head of a hawk with beak and eye.
When I looked above the trees, a hawk flew there.
On a walk I found a large feather.

That Was Never There Before

Let us cut the end out of the book
And take it, hide it now for when we most need

—Judith Hall, "A Book Cut and Left in the Forest"

They come at night—
the old ones from those agency prisons and boarding schools.
They walk the sky carrying northern lights.
Maybe they're looking for a road.
Maybe they're hungry for turtle meat.
Maybe they want to pick up a rock or just smell the earth.
They shake their heads—Why haven't we learned it right?
They can't leave us alone, or let go.
They're meddlers. Interferers with the lights.
Here—over this way—put your thumb in our socket—
see how *you* dance to this new light.

The Messianic Craze at Chibity

Spirits came from the book the missionaries gave us.

They brought supper on metal plates that did not break
when we tossed them against the wall.

They told us to follow Jesus's tracks.
He had his spelling lessons already done.
He rode a canoe.
He gave us a world we didn't know until we were there.

She said she wouldn't be long.
But it was years before she came back.
And when she did, we didn't know who she was.
She'd been a mother, she said.
But now she was someone we could pass
in an old yellow Buick with mud flaps,
the kind that took a tank of gasoline to get to the next block.
You can't ignore me, she said.
We can't act like we've been with you all those years.
What could we do?
The mission school was our lawn.

They Said Hallelujah

The missionaries said he was seated on his throne. The wounded got up from the ground. He made them whole and it happened before our eyes. We had not seen this before, though the missionaries said he would. He is a God who robs his people of what they are and want to be and makes them into sheep. We wanted to be warriors and did not want to bleat. Then the ones we looked for brought us whiskey. It was something we had to have to survive as sheep.

Pencil Factory, Est. 1972, Blackfeet Reservation

The message came by the carriers
of books, pamphlets, primers.
These government reports were exportations of our events
to a government far away.

I discovered the classroom was a strong drink of whiskey—
method and theory deadened the wounds.

Teaching was a song of alcohol—
silver rockets in the glare.

Postscript:
In the old days we covered our bare chest with a buffalo robe
and did not feel the cold. In the drafty schoolrooms dressed in
wool, we felt the cold.

Case Load: The Drive across the State Line to Nebraska for
    Alcohol

American Indian women are twice as likely to be sexually assaulted as
women generally, and the isolation of the reservation life makes the odds
worse still.

—*Christian Century*, July 11, 2012

We drive a few miles south on highway 407 from Pine Ridge to Nebraska.
We load a case into our trunk—drive back to South Dakota—slowly—to
avoid arrest. We know we could be stopped. Yet we kept driving when
the highway patrol passed—who would have discovered our cargo—as if
he didn't know it was there already. We were not fully sober, but not yet
drunk—yelping about battles we had never known—yet knew were
there—writing our own citation of labeled cases—then blotting out all
that happened—taking it back as a report to our own department of the
interior.

The New Square Sun

He . . . opened their ears in oppression.

—Job 36:15

The missionaries opened the book and light came from it. An old one
stood on the edge of the room. Nearly inside the wall. His body stiff as a
pencil. His hair the color of lead. A feather eraser—if he turned his head.
It was the new sun dance—staring into the book until we walked with
the words—until we could write their weight. The wingless. The
heartless. It's why everything had to be ripped. They will be mad to hear.
And I am mad to say.

The Hunt

The cold floors of the schoolroom.
The standing walls—
cliffs they were.

I was given a book to read from in front of others
but words ran across the page.

I went inland—
they followed
tracking the animal
sending pelt, paws, ears, tail, meat
from the room in pieces.

Outside the wind howled.
The snow was chicken white.

Surrender

I had to act like I wanted to be there—
like I was grateful for the hurting.

Once again in front of
others I read with charity to show
how pitiful the pupil
how invited to be something to be remade.

They demolished a sense of self and sent the fragments broken
into the world.

I still wake with my hands clawed.
The room smells of tears.

The pages were tongues that licked the wounds.

Life after Death in the Person of a Shepherd

When I read the Bible stories the stories came off
the page. The words of the stories wore robes
and turbans. They pounded sandals from bark though
bark was not in the desert or not much of it. But the
words said bark and the bark was there with
animal sinew to tie around their ankles. The words
about flocks became sheep. The words also were
shepherds. Or one shepherd in particular. The words
wandered in the wilderness. When they were
thirsty they said water. A word held a video camera.
A word chased a lizard across a rock. It became
a living show. Why would a word want to be on a
page white as silence? A word pauses. It looks up.
Adjusts its sunglasses. How did words not go blind
with brightness?

Could There Have Been Another Way?

[It] is a land for cattle and your servants have cattle.

—Numbers 32:4

They counted their men of war in ranks and formations in walled forts. They rode through the land with their railcars, their highways and suburbs. They were an army of pencils and papers stuck in a book that said, here read, be as one of us who reads. It is a country you may enter because you know the words.

THE ORIGIN OF LAW

⸻ ⚬⚬⚬ ⸻

Spotted Cloud Elementary, 2012

Characters:
TEACHER
THE BUFFALO

Setting:
the Spotted Cloud gymnasium
a bench in the middle of the floor

The Origin of Law

TEACHER
At one time, the buffalo lived in the middle of the World.
I'm not sure where that was—probably the buffalo didn't either.
But somehow they came from the middle of the World to the middle
of the Great Plains of America before it was America.
The Maker created it for the buffalo.
They were the reason for the land to be land.

The Buffalo wander onto the stage. They paw the ground. Snort.
One scratches himself with his hind leg. They eat grass.

TEACHER
The Maker created the buffalo for the early people that were on the land.
The buffalo were everything the people needed.
They were hide and meat and medicine. They were spirit and law.
The buffalo herds were sheriff and posse of the plains.

THE BUFFALO
I'm the boss.
I'm the boss.
We're the boss.

TEACHER
The buffalo had roamed in the middle of the World
after The Maker first formed them.
Now they came to Earth because the early people needed them.
The early people spoke.
They said, Where's hide for teepees? Where's meat? Where's medicine?

Then the early people saw the buffalo.

THE BUFFALO
We're meat.
We're hide.

TEACHER
And they shot the buffalo with their arrows.

THE BUFFALO
Ouch!
Ouch!

TEACHER
The early people looked at the buffalo fallen on the prairie.
They thanked the buffalo for their lives.

THE BUFFALO
Because the early people were thankful, they became human beings.

TEACHER
But the buffalo did not like being shot. They called a buffalo council.

THE BUFFALO
What will we do with these people?
Let's run from them.
We will give them the hunt, as all human beings need something to hunt.
It is purpose for their lives.
We'll run fast.
Yes.
We run fast.

As long as the people honor us, the land will be strong.
Our honor is their honor. We give them a way to live.
They need us.
They need us.
We are the origin of law. We are the Law!—

TEACHER
Once, a Buffalo came to the early people and transformed into a Human
Being, and gave the early people ceremonies to follow.
They were a code of behavior for their survival.
They would enable the early people to remain human beings.

They were called Vision Quest.
They were called Sun Dance.
They were called Sweat Lodge.
The ceremonies showed the early people how to respect themselves and
The Maker.

The buffalo sit on the bench and take notes.

TEACHER
The ceremonies showed the early people responsibility
and self-governance or sovereignty.
You know how trouble comes from within and without.
The ceremonies showed the early people how to govern trouble.
There are reasons for ceremonies.
There are reasons for codes of behavior.
There are reasons for law.
It's not easy, you see.
The ceremonies were given to the early people
so they would not destroy their families and themselves.
We have something inside us that is not from The Maker—something
that causes trouble.

Still, the early people argued—Law? Who needs law? Not us. Not us.

The buffalo stand and talk in their small discussion group.

TEACHER
The people don't know what to do.
They have no inner compass except to get in trouble, and then regret it.
They live for themselves.
Sometimes they are good.
Their duplicity is the need for law.
But we showed them how to work as a group.
Otherwise they do despicable things.
Like what?
Like what?
Go to war against themselves and others.

Destroy what is good for them.

TEACHER
That's the origin of law.
It is what we must do to be human beings on this earth.
Otherwise there's punishment.

THE BUFFALO
Is there anything as angry as a buffalo?
Is there anything as bad as a buffalo?

TEACHER
The buffalo were satisfied with themselves.
They thought the whole World should have been called Buffalo.
The Universe should have been called Buffalo.
But The Maker liked differences.
He tilted the earth and some of the people from another place
fell onto the shore.
Their little ships lined up like a flock of migrating birds.
Now the later people are everywhere.

THE BUFFALO
They send their cavalry.
They build forts.

The buffalo turn the bench on its side, as though the wall of a fort.
They hide behind it, looking over the wall.

Now their little floppy wagons hop over the land.
They are shooting the early people.
The early people are shooting back.
The later people build straight lines on the land.
They make rails for their wagons that hold their hands together
and walk as one.

TEACHER
Now the later people shoot the buffalo.

The buffalo jump up from behind the bench.

TEACHER
They shoot from passing trains. The buffalo are piled high on the prairie.
The later people keep shooting.

The buffalo lie on the stage with their legs stiff in the air.

TEACHER
Now the buffalo are dead.

THE BUFFALO
I am not dead.
I am not dead.

The buffalo rise and recite "The Rising of the Buffalo Men"—

I rise, I rise.
I, whose tread makes the earth to rumble.

I rise, I rise.
I, in whose thighs there is strength.

I rise, I rise.
I, who whips his back with his tail when in a rage.

I rise, I rise.
I, in whose humped shoulder there is power.

I rise, I rise.
I, who shakes his head when angered.

I rise, I rise.
I, whose horns are sharp and curved.

*Now there is a "soundscape" with great clatter and flurry. The buffalo turn
    the bench right-side up and sit.*

TEACHER
From the Afterworld, the buffalo come in the thunder and lightning.

The buffalo clap their thighs with their hands, making the sound of thunder.

TEACHER
They jump from the sky in tornados.

The buffalo stand on the bench and jump off.

TEACHER
The sound of their hooves sends the people running.

The buffalo stomp their feet, running in place.

TEACHER
They stampede in sandstorms and cause drought.

The buffalo make a shuuuuuuuuuu sound for the wind and blowing sand.

TEACHER
They rock the sea with hurricanes.

The buffalo rub their hands back and forth on their thighs for the sound of surf.

TEACHER
They rumble the middle of the World and there are earthquakes.

The buffalo rattle the bench on the floor.

TEACHER
They snort and there are volcanoes.

The buffalo lift the lectern as if it is a mountain, and make a spewing sound.

TEACHER
They batter the sky with meteor showers.

The buffalo pound the bench with their hands.

TEACHER
The buffalo invade our stories.
They become the subject of lectures.
They are writing their own book.
They wait for you on the highway in patrol cars.
They sit as judges in the courts of law.
They visit their relatives in Yellowstone Park.
It is the buffalo that speak in your heart.

Postscript:
Acknowledgment for the spirit of the piece to Francis La Flesche, Omaha
(1857–1932), first native ethnologist, who worked with the anthropologist
Alice Fletcher, recording the prayers and songs of Indian tribes.

"The Rising of the Buffalo Men" is one of the prayers/songs he recorded.

Francis La Flesche, *The Osage Tribe: The Rite of Vigil*, 39th Annual
Report, Bureau of American Ethnology, Washington, D.C., 1925 (found
in an old paperback by A. Grove Day, *The Sky Clears: Poetry of the
American Indians*, University of Nebraska Press, 1951).

In the book. La Flesche also gives the native *clipped* version of the prayer/
song:

He-Whose-Tread-Makes-the-Earth-Rumble.
Great-thighs.
Tail-Curved.
Back-Humped-Shoulder.
Shakes-His-Head.
Curved-Horns.

Bless him.

Acknowledgments

The author wishes to thank the following publications in which some of the poems in this collection previously appeared:

Adroit: "Report (1)"

Caliban: "Fort Yates' Infirmary," "The Spirit of Bull Head's Wife Visits the National Gallery," "Bull Head's Wife Opens Ristorante Hortense Fiquet," "Bull Head's Wife Studies Frances Glessner Lee," and "Nutshell Studies of Unexplained Death"

I-70: "Wolf Dreaming" and "Life after Death in the Person of a Shepherd"

Lightning Key Review: A Magazine for Narrative: "In Winter the Storm Wind Rattles the Weather Stripping of the Door"

Midway Journal: "Bull Head's Wife on the Eighty-Mile Journey," "Military Honors at Fort Yates," and "Bull Head's Wife Mail-Orders at the Telegraph Office"

Paddlefish: "Report on Indian Education from the Indian"

Platt River Review: "No More Stories Told by the Voice," "The Train Tracks," and "That Was Never There Before"

Saranac Review: "Spotted Tail's Daughter"

Solstice: A Magazine of Diverse Voices: "That Was Never There Before," "They Said Hallelujah," and "Pencil Factory, Est. 1972, Blackfeet Reservation"

Toe Good Poetry: "Those Old Voices Always Are with Me"

WITNESS, Childhood in America Issue: "The Shootings at Red Lake Reservation" (published under the title "Red Lake")

The author also wishes to thank the following anthologies in which some of the poems in this collection previously appeared:

County Lines, 87 Minnesota Counties, 130 Minnesota poets (Bemidji, MN: Loonfeather Press, 2008): "The Shootings at Red Lake Reservation"

Encore: Prize Poems of the NFSPS 2012 (NFSPS, 2012): "What Shape Did You Take?"

Grist: 2002 Anthology of Missouri State Poetry Society, edited by Tom Padgett, Sandra L. Brown, and the Missouri State Poetry Society (Bolivar,

MO: Barn Owl Press, 2002): "First Train from North Dakota to Carlisle Indian Industrial School"

Open to Interpretation: Intimate Landscapes, edited by Patrick Thomas (Minneapolis, MN: Milkweed Editions, 2012): "Too Hard to Forget" (published under the title "Volumes")

Additionally, "The Origin of Law" was performed at the *Native Voices Short Play Festival* (Autry National Center, Los Angeles, CA), where it won the 2013 Von Marie Atchley Excellence in Playwriting Award. It was also presented at Survival of the First Voices Festival, 2014, San Juan College, Farmington, New Mexico, by Near Water Theatre Group.

The author extends further acknowledgments to: Barbara Landis for the *Indian Helper*, the Carlisle Indian Industrial School Newspaper; James Schaap for an article on Bull Head; Clark Whitehorn for direction in development of the manuscript; and news articles on the 2005 Red Lake Shootings that appeared in the Minneapolis *Star Tribune*, the St. Paul *Pioneer Press*, and the *New York Times*; and Jodi Rave's articles in the *Missoulian*.

Finally, the author is grateful for a 2009 Expressive Arts Grant through the National Museum of the American Indian in Washington, D.C., for research on the history of native education.

Bibliography

Adams, Evelyn C. *American Indian Education: Government Schools and Economic Progress.* New York: Arno Press, 1971.

Harkins, Arthur M. *Public Education on a Minnesota Chippewa Reservation; Final Report Conducted by Arthur M. Harkins, Under the Supervision of Rosalie H. Wax.* Lawrence: University of Kansas, 1968.

Jones, W. A. Annual Reports of the Department of the Interior for the Fiscal Year Ended June 30, 1898. Washington, D.C.: Government Printing Office, 1898.

Powell, J. W. Seventh Annual Report, Bureau of Ethnology to the Secretary of the Smithsonian Institution, 1885–86. Washington, D.C.: Government Printing Office, 1891.

Senese, Guy B. *Self-Determination and the Social Education of Native Americans.* New York: Praeger, 1991.

Szasz, Margaret Connell. *Education and the American Indian: The Road to Self-Determination, 1928–1973.* Albuquerque: University of New Mexico Press, 1974.

———. *Indian Education in the American Colonies, 1607–1783.* Albuquerque: University of New Mexico Press, 1988.